THE USPC G[...]

BANDAGING

YOUR

HORSE

ALSO BY SUSAN E. HARRIS

THE USPC GUIDE TO
BANDAGING
YOUR
HORSE

written and illustrated by

SUSAN E. HARRIS

RUTH RING HARVIE, USPC EDITOR

Howell Book House
New York

Copyright © 1997 by Susan E. Harris and The United States Pony Clubs, Inc.

All rights reserved. No part of this book may be reproduced or transmitted in any form by any means, electronic or mechanical, including photocopying, recording, or by any information storage and retrieval system, without permission in writing from the Publisher.

Howell Book House
A Simon and Schuster Macmillan Company
1633 Broadway
New York, NY 10019

MACMILLAN is a registered trademark of Macmillan, Inc.

Library of Congress Cataloging-in-Publication Data

Harris, Susan E.
    The USPC guide to bandaging your horse / written and illustrated by Susan E. Harris :
  Ruth Ring Harvie, USPC editor.
      p.   cm.
    ISBN 0-86705-638-9
    1. Horses—Wounds and Injuries—Prevention. 2. Leg—Wounds and injuries—
Prevention. 3. Foot—Wounds and injuries—Prevention. 4. Leg—Care and
hygiene. 5. Foot—Care and hygiene. 6. Bandages and bandaging. I. Harvie,
Ruth Ring. II. United States Pony Clubs. III. Title.
SF959.L42H37   1997
636.1'089758052—dc21   97-19351
                                             CIP

10 9 8 7 6 5 4 3 2

CONTENTS

ABOUT THE UNITED STATES PONY CLUBS, INC.

The United States Pony Clubs, Inc. is an educational youth organization that teaches riding, mounted sports, and the care of horses and ponies, and develops in youth the characteristics of responsibility, sportsmanship, moral judgment, leadership, and self-confidence.

Since its beginning in Great Britain in 1928, Pony Club has become the largest junior equestrian group in the world, with more than 125,000 members in 27 countries. At this writing, the U.S. Pony Clubs have approximately 11,000 members in more than 500 clubs. Members ride mounts of all breeds and sizes, not just ponies; the term "pony" originally referred to any mount ridden by a young person.

The U.S. Pony Clubs teach a curriculum which covers balanced seat horsemanship on the flat, over fences, and in the open, along with safety, knowledge, and practical skills in horse care and management. The goal is to produce safe, happy, and confident horsepersons, who can ride, handle, and care for their horse and equipment competently at their level, with an understanding of the reasons for what they do.

Pony Clubbers progress at their own pace through a series of levels or ratings, from D (basic) through C (intermediate) to B, HA, and A (advanced). The requirements for each rating are called the USPC Standards of Proficiency. The lower level ratings (D-1 through C-2) are tested within the local Pony Club; the C-3 rating is tested at a Regional Testing; and the B, HA, and A levels are national ratings, requiring advanced levels of knowledge, horsemanship, and horse care and management skills.

Besides instruction and ratings, Pony Club offers activities such as Combined Training, Foxhunting, Dressage, Mounted Games, Show Jumping, Tetrathlon, and Vaulting, with emphasis on safety, teamwork, and good horsemanship and sportsmanship.

For more information about the U.S. Pony Clubs, please contact:

United States Pony Clubs, Inc.
The Kentucky Horse Park
Iron Works Pike
Lexington, KY 40511
(606) 254-PONY (7669)

INTRODUCTION

A horse's legs are among the most important parts of his body—and also the most vulnerable to injury. Proper leg care and protection, including bandaging when appropriate, is essential in keeping a horse sound, willing, and able to do his work.

Bandaging (also called wrapping) is an important skill for any horseperson. Knowing when and how to bandage can make the difference between a sound, comfortable horse and an unsound, hurting horse. You may need to bandage your horse's legs for protection, for warmth and comfort, to treat an injury, or to prevent swelling. Tail wraps may also be used for protection or to shape the tail for formal turnout occasions. Leg boots are often used instead of bandages for protection during exercise, turnout, and shipping.

This book covers different types of boots and bandages, their purposes, the materials used, and how to apply them. It also includes tips on when to bandage, maintaining boots and bandages, and keeping your horse's legs sound. This book complies with U.S. Pony Club Standards and requirements for passing Pony Club rating tests in bandaging and leg care, but it will also be helpful for anyone who owns, rides, or cares for horses, and wants to keep his horse's legs sound.

CAUTION: While bandaging can be helpful when done correctly, improper bandaging can cause serious harm to your horse. You must learn when to bandage, what type of bandage to use, and how to apply it correctly. This takes care, practice, and hands-on instruction from an expert; it cannot be learned just by reading a book. It is better not to bandage at all than to bandage incorrectly and risk hurting your horse.

THE USPC GUIDE TO

BANDAGING

YOUR

HORSE

KEEPING YOUR HORSE'S LEGS SOUND

Your horse's legs are among the most important—and most vulnerable—parts of his body. Because such essential structures as bones, tendons, and ligaments are close to the surface, covered only by skin, they are at risk to injury from bumps and bangs. The lower leg structure is a complex system with many functions and is subject to athletic injuries due to stress, strains, sprains, and overwork.

GET TO KNOW YOUR HORSE'S LEGS

You should learn the parts and basic structures of the horse's lower leg. (For more information on horse leg anatomy, see *The United States Pony Club Manual of Horsemanship: Advanced Horsemanship* [Book 3], page 251.) Make it a habit to look at and palpate (feel) your horse's legs every day, before and after you ride him. Know how his legs normally look and feel, including any blemishes, scars, or chronic conditions he may have. This way, you can immediately spot any changes and treat minor problems before they become serious. It's especially important to check your horse's legs and feet and jog him out to detect any stiffness or lameness the day after a competition or strenuous workout.

If you notice any of the following (or any other problem), check it out immediately. Ask your instructor for advice, or consult your veterinarian and/or your farrier. Don't wait to see if it gets worse!

Structures of the lower leg.

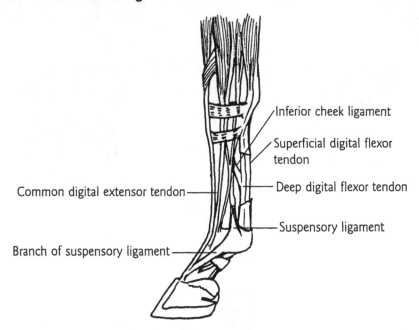

Inferior cheek ligament

Superficial digital flexor tendon

Common digital extensor tendon

Deep digital flexor tendon

Suspensory ligament

Branch of suspensory ligament

Exterior of the lower leg.

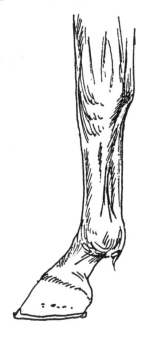

- Cuts, scrapes, or skin irritations.

- Interference marks: Cuts, bruises, or scuffed hair on the inside of the fetlock joint may show that the horse is interfering, or striking one leg with the opposite foot as he moves. Be sure to point these out to your farrier, as corrective shoeing may help.

- Heat: A part of a leg that is abnormally hot may be inflamed or injured, especially if it is also puffy or tender.

- Swelling: A hot, tender swelling indicates a strain, sprain, bruise, infection, or other injury. A cool, puffy swelling that "pits" (leaves an indentation) when pressed with a finger may indicate edema, or fluid collected in the soft tissues.

- Filling: A swelling that "fills in" the grooves that normally show around tendons and ligaments may be an early sign of stress or injury to the tendons or suspensory ligament.

- Stocking up: A swelling of all four legs or both hind legs, caused by poor circulation and/or lack of exercise. It is cool, painless, and usually goes down with gentle exercise. Stocking up is more common in older horses and in horses kept in stalls.

- Lameness, stiffness, or favoring one leg: It is normal for a horse to rest one hind leg, but resting or "pointing" a front leg is usually a sign of a foot or leg problem. (For more about recognizing lameness, see *The United Pony Club Manual of Horsemanship: Basics for Beginners* [Book 1], page 212.)

Signs of leg problems.

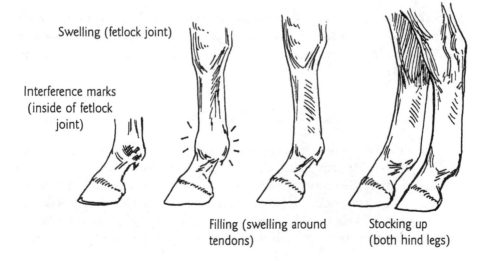

Swelling (fetlock joint)

Interference marks (inside of fetlock joint)

Filling (swelling around tendons)

Stocking up (both hind legs)

EXERCISE DAILY, BUT DON'T OVERWORK

Horses' legs need daily exercise to function well. Standing in a stall for long periods, especially on a hard surface with insufficient bedding, is hard on the legs and joints and can lead to unfitness, stiffness, and stocking up. Stabled horses need exercise or turnout time every day.

Excessive work, especially doing more work than the horse is fit for, can cause stress, injury, and unsoundness. Many serious injuries occur when the muscles are fatigued and the structures of the leg lose their normal strength, elasticity, and coordination.

WARM UP, WARM DOWN, AND COOL OUT

A horse's muscles, tendons, ligaments, and joints need to warm up slowly before being subjected to fast or strenuous work, in order to prevent injury. This is especially important for stabled horses, older horses, and stiff or arthritic horses. Always walk for the first 10 to 15 minutes, then gradually increase the exercise, trotting and cantering in both directions, especially before jumping. At the end of every ride, warm down by gradually reducing the level of exercise, then walk until your horse is cool. This helps his circulation return to normal after exercise.

Careful, conscientious warming up, warming down, and cooling out are among the most important things you can do to protect your horse's soundness.

Working a horse (especially jumping) without warming up properly first, puts him at risk of injury.

TRIMMING AND SHOEING

Proper hoof trimming and/or shoeing, on a regular schedule, protect your horse's legs as well as keep his feet comfortable. Loose or overgrown shoes, unbalanced feet, and especially feet with long toes and low heels, put excessive stress on the flexor tendons and can lead to tripping, stumbling, and injuries.

LEG PROTECTION

Boots or properly applied bandages can help prevent certain injuries. Horses that are prone to interfere, especially young horses or those with crooked legs, should wear protective boots or exercise bandages (the latter must be put on by an expert). Boots or exercise bandages should also be used for activities during which a horse is likely to strike himself, such as longeing, lateral work, or fast work. Bell boots protect the heels from overreaching injuries or "grabs" during jumping, in muddy footing, or on horses that forge. Shipping boots or bandages protect the legs during travel, and stable bandages are sometimes used to prevent leg injuries in the stall, especially when stabling in temporary stalls where there is a greater risk of injury than at home.

BOOTS AND BANDAGES

Boots, and especially bandages, *must* be applied correctly or they may cause injury instead of protecting the legs. The greatest danger is bandaging too tightly or with uneven pressure, which can compress the blood vessels, interfere with circulation, and put excessive pressure on tendons and other structures. Improperly fastened boots or exercise bandages may come undone during exercise and cause the horse to trip or stumble.

TYPES AND PURPOSES OF BANDAGES

Bandages can provide protection against injuries, especially when transporting a horse or during activities such as longeing or jumping. As a veterinary aid, they are used to protect a wound or to treat sprains, strains, or swelling. The basic types of bandages are:

- *Shipping bandages:* To prevent swelling of the legs and for protection against bumps and scrapes during loading, unloading, and travel.

- *Stable bandages:* For warmth and protection in the stall, and to prevent swelling of the legs after hard work. Also used to dry wet or muddy legs.

- *Exercise bandages:* For protection against blows, overreaching, and interfering; to absorb energy and to prevent hyperextension (excessive stretching) of the fetlock joint during work.

- *Treatment bandages:* To prevent and reduce swelling, to cover a wound or hold a dressing in place, to limit the range of motion of an injured leg or joint, and for specialized treatment of injuries or unsoundnesses.

- *Tail bandages:* For protection of the tail during shipping, breeding, or foaling, to protect a braided tail, or to shape the hair of the dock.

CAUTIONS ABOUT BANDAGING

All bandages must be applied correctly, or they may do more harm than good. Uneven pressure from a poorly applied bandage or a tight ring of pressure around a leg can damage a horse's tendons. This is called cording a leg and can result in lameness or even a bowed tendon. Bandages and bandage fastenings must be put on evenly and with the right amount of pressure.

Always use enough leg padding to distribute the pressure evenly around the structures and contours of the leg. Insufficient padding can cause damage to tendons, skin, and bony prominences around joints, and can result in cording and lameness. Padding must be clean, smooth, and free from lumps, wrinkles, and straw or other debris.

A bandage must be fastened correctly, or it may come loose and trip the horse. This is especially important for exercise bandages, which should be sewn down when used for galloping or jumping. Fasteners must not be applied so as to indent the bandage or create a continuous ring of pressure around the leg or tail.

If, after removing a bandage, the tendons appear swollen, puffy, or have a rippled appearance, this may be a sign of cording, or inflammation of the tendons or tendon sheath, due to improper bandaging.

Bandaging is a skill that requires practice, experience, and attention to details. Do not try to apply a bandage until you have had hands-on instruction from someone who is experienced in bandaging correctly. Certain special-purpose bandages, such as an immobilizing bandage, should be applied only under the supervision of a veterinarian. Always follow your veterinarian's instructions regarding bandages.

Signs of cording.

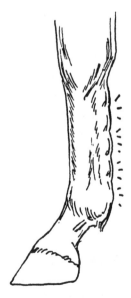

Rippled appearance of tendons: a sign of tendon damage caused by improper bandaging.

MATERIALS FOR BANDAGING

Bandages are made up of leg wraps, padding, and fasteners. Some bandages also use a dressing to cover a wound or hold medication. There are many types of bandage materials for different purposes. In Pony Club, for example, certain kinds are preferred. These have been found to be the safest and most suitable for the kind of bandaging Pony Clubbers (and most other horse owners) do, and are less likely to cause damage to horses' legs.

Bandage materials should be clean, smooth, comfortable for the horse, and a suitable size and material for the purpose of the bandage. They should conform to the shape of the leg without creating lumps or wrinkles, which can result in uneven pressure and damage to the leg. It helps if they are inexpensive, easy to obtain, and reusable.

LEG WRAPS OR BANDAGES

Leg wraps or bandages are usually 4 to 6 inches wide and from 10 to 16 feet long, depending on the size of the horse. They should be made of washable material. If they are made from a material that has some ability to stretch, they will conform to the shape of the leg more easily. Bandages must be tightly rolled before use.

TYPES OF LEG WRAPS

Flannel bandages: Made of heavy double-sided flannel napped on one or both sides, flannel bandages are strong, easy to launder, and inexpensive. Flannel does not stretch or conform easily to the shape of the leg. Flannel bandages should be washed and hung out to dry smoothly before using them the first time; otherwise they can be stiff and unwieldy to use.

Flannel bandages can be bought ready-made, or you can buy the material by the yard and tear it into strips of the proper length and width. For small ponies, strips should be 4 inches wide and about 14 feet long. Bandages for small horses should be 5 or 6 inches wide and 15 feet long; for large horses, strips should be 6 inches wide and 17 feet long, especially for shipping bandages, which require extra length.

Knit, stockinette, or track bandages: Made of cotton knit (stockinette) or polyester double-knit, which has some ability to stretch and conform to the shape of the leg, particularly when new. They are available in widths of 4 to 6 inches and in lengths of 7 to 10 feet. Most have Velcro® fasteners sewn onto one end. Do not use the type with narrow tie tapes because they can cause pressure damage to a horse's leg; if your bandages have tapes, they should be cut off. (See fasteners, page 15.)

Most cotton-knit bandages are too short and too narrow for use as shipping bandages, especially if they have shrunk from use and washing. Two bandages sewn together end to end will make one bandage of the right length for a shipping wrap. Some polyester knit bandages are long enough to use as shipping wraps for ponies or small horses.

Knit bandages, in particular cotton stockinette, tend to shrink if laundered in hot water or put in a dryer. Polyester bandages are less likely to shrink.

Fleece bandages (polo wraps) should not be used as a substitute for flannel or knit leg wraps. They are usually too short to be used effectively over leg padding, and their surface picks up bedding and other debris.

SPECIAL-PURPOSE BANDAGES AND WRAPS

Many other types of bandages are made for special purposes, such as treatment bandages or exercise wraps. Don't use them without assistance from your instructor or veterinarian, as certain bandage materials make it easy to cause damage to a horse's tendons if not used properly.

Polo wraps (fleece or Sandown bandages): Bandages made of washable, slightly stretchy polyester fleece, with Velcro fasteners.

Polo wraps are often used in place of brushing boots or exercise bandages during work, longeing, and turnout. They are popular because they come in many attractive colors, are easy to wash, and are convenient to apply.

Polo wraps have some serious drawbacks. They are designed to be used without padding underneath, which can result in excessive pressure on the tendons. If the Velcro fasteners are applied too tightly or always at the same spot, they can cause cording, or tendon damage. Polo wraps absorb water; they become heavy, sag, and slip when wet, even when reinforced with pins and/or sewn ends. This makes them unsafe for cross-country work or in wet conditions. A scientific study by veterinarians has shown that polo wraps offer inferior protection to correctly applied exercise bandages or sport-medicine boots.

Because of the above drawbacks, polo wraps are not permitted in U.S. Pony Club rating tests or competitions. If your horse needs leg protection while being ridden, properly fitted boots or exercise bandages (put on by an experienced person) are preferred instead of polo wraps.

Foam-padded elastic bandage: A specialty bandage with foam rubber self-adhering to the inside of the elastic, used for exercise bandages.

Saratoga® bandages: Bandages with elastic woven into the material and a slightly rubberized backing to prevent slipping during use. They are used for exercise bandages over cotton or foam leg padding. Because they do not absorb water, they are suitable for work in wet conditions.

Elastic crepe bandage (VetRap® and other brands): Self-adhering lightweight elastic crepe bandage which conforms easily to the shape of the leg or foot. It is excellent for hoof wraps, pressure bandages, and bandaging hard-to-reach areas such as heel grabs. Crepe bandages can be reused once or twice if removed carefully.

Ace® bandage: Elastic bandage sold in drugstores and tack shops. Because it is very stretchy, care must be taken not to pull it tightly enough to cut off circulation. The 6-inch width works well with an ice pack, as it will contract as the ice melts. Narrower widths are sometimes used for tail bandages, especially after the bandage has lost some of its elasticity through repeated use and washing.

Conforming gauze: Gauze rolls of various widths, slightly stretchy. It conforms gently to the contours of even hard-to-bandage areas and is used to hold wound dressings in place. This material can bind, rub, or cause cording if applied incorrectly.

Super K VetRap®: Synthetic cotton roll which can be rolled over a dressing to hold it in place over a wound or provide padding, particularly on hard-to-bandage places such as joints or pasterns. It is not sturdy enough to be used as an outside wrap.

Elastic adhesive bandage (Elastoplast®, Elastikon®, and other brands): A strong elastic bandage with adhesive on the inside surface, available from veterinarians, drugstores, and tack shops. It is used mainly for bandaging wounds and can be used to wrap around a foot that has thrown a shoe, to prevent the wall from chipping until the shoe can be replaced.

Duct tape: Strong, waterproof, adhesive repair tape sold in hardware stores. It can be used to wrap around a foot that has lost a shoe to prevent the wall from chipping until the shoe can be replaced, or to protect and reinforce the bottom of a hoof bandage. Because duct tape can bind and cause cording or pressure damage, it should be used only on the hoof, not on the coronary band or any part of the leg.

Gel packs and cooling wraps: These items, made of a special gel which retains cold, can be cooled in a freezer and applied in place of an ice pack.

Types of bandages.

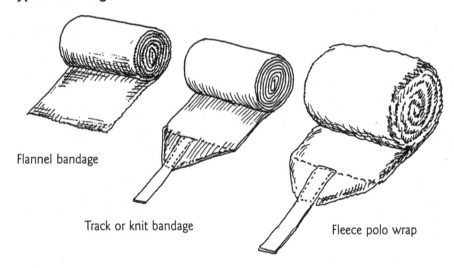

Flannel bandage

Track or knit bandage

Fleece polo wrap

LEG PADS AND OTHER PADDING MATERIALS

A leg bandage must *always* be applied over adequate padding. The padding distributes the pressure evenly and is compressed so that it fits snugly against the structures of the leg, giving gentle support to the tissues. Padding must be soft and smooth against the leg, and thick enough to distribute pressure evenly, without binding or causing too much pressure on a tendon, joint, or bony prominence. Lumps, wrinkles, or hard ridges next to the leg can create a pressure point and interfere with circulation.

The size and thickness of the padding depend on the size of the horse's leg and the type of bandage applied. Leg pads are usually about 14 to 18 inches high and 18 to 24 inches long.

Some synthetic materials, and in particular foams, may cause the legs to sweat, especially in hot weather. It is better to use a breathable, absorbent material such as cotton or cotton terry cloth next to the leg, instead of foam rubber or synthetic foam.

Some types of leg padding materials are machine washable; others are not. All will last longer if they are kept as clean as possible and stored in a clean place. Keep leg pads rolled in the direction in which they are used, to help preserve their shape.

Leg pads and padding materials can be obtained from tack stores or veterinary supply catalogs. Some can be purchased ready-made; others must be made up from various kinds of padding materials.

TYPES OF LEG PADDING

Sheet cotton: Preferred for use in Pony Club because it is soft, clean, inexpensive, and can be made to any size and thickness required. It comes in folded sheets and must be made up into leg pads.

Cotton leg pads may be used many times if they are handled carefully. However, they are not washable and must be discarded when they become soiled, lumpy, or uneven.

Polyester or cotton-polyester quilt batting: Can be made into leg pads of the proper size and thickness for stable bandages or shipping bandages. Polyester batting can be machine washed and dried, but cotton-polyester batting is not washable and should be treated as sheet cotton.

Ready-made cotton leg quilts: Quilted cotton pads, available from tack shops and stable supply catalogs, are durable and machine washable. They are usually too short for shipping bandages, however, and the sewn seams or binding may create pressure points and prevent the pad from conforming to the leg.

Ready-made leg pads: Ready-made leg pads are sold in tack shops. They come in a variety of materials, including polyester, cotton sheets covered with cheesecloth, synthetic felt, and combinations with a layer of foam rubber. "Pillow" pads are extra long, thick, and puffy but may not be tall enough for shipping bandages. Most types are machine washable.

Kendall Cottons®: A brand of synthetic cotton, nylon-reinforced for durability, that is sold in sheets about 1/8-inch thick. The material conforms to the leg, can be cut to size, and can be rinsed carefully. Kendall cottons can be used to cover dressings and as leg pads for exercise bandages, but several layers are necessary for stable or shipping bandages. Be sure to use enough padding and avoid wrinkles.

Fybagee® pads: A brand of leg pads, made with synthetic cotton felt on the outside and a thin layer of foam inside. These pads are washable and may be cut to size but do not conform to the leg very well. They are useful as padding under exercise bandages.

Types of leg pads.

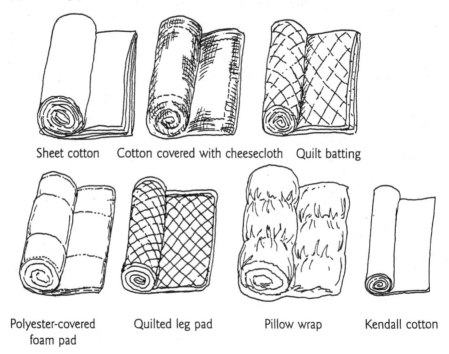

Sheet cotton   Cotton covered with cheesecloth   Quilt batting

Polyester-covered foam pad   Quilted leg pad   Pillow wrap   Kendall cotton

MAKING YOUR OWN LEG PADS

You can make pads to fit your horse's legs and the type of bandage you need to apply. In addition, they will be less expensive than buying ready-made pads.

Measure your horse's legs (from the ground to the base of the knee and hock) before buying (or cutting) padding material. For a shipping bandage, the pad should reach from the ground to an inch above the bottom of the hock or knee joint. For a standing bandage, it should be slightly shorter: from the hock or knee joint to the coronary band. Pads for exercise bandages are shorter (from the base of the knee or hock to the bottom of the fetlock joint), and the padding is thinner than for shipping or standing bandages.

Sheet cotton leg pads: Sheet cottons come folded in half, lengthwise. The number of sheets needed, the way they are folded, and the thickness and shape of the leg pad depends on the type of bandage, the area it must cover, and the size of the horse's leg.

Making your own leg pads.

Measure for leg pad size.

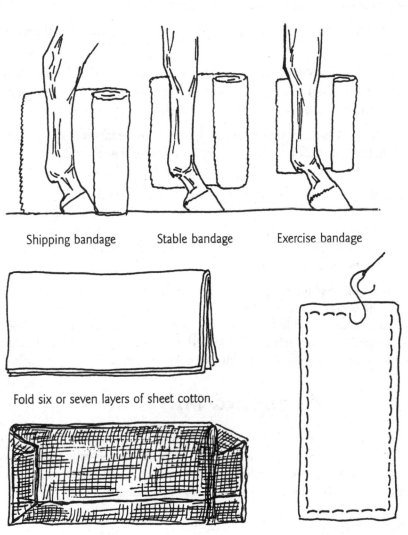

Shipping bandage　　Stable bandage　　Exercise bandage

Fold six or seven layers of sheet cotton.

Cover with cheesecloth.

Stitch layers together.

To make a basic cotton leg pad, use six to eight sheets of cotton, folded length-wise. For larger horses, hind leg pads, or pads for shipping bandages, use seven or eight sheets and fold them across the width to make them taller.

When folding and fitting sheet-cotton leg pads, make sure the padding is of a uniform thickness, without lumps, holes, or wrinkles. After you have assembled a leg pad and checked its fit, you can bind the layers together to make them more durable and easier to handle. You can do this in several ways:

1. Stitch the layers of sheet cotton together, using large stitches through all layers.

2. Cover the completed leg pad with cheesecloth. Secure the cheesecloth by stitching through the leg pad, as above, or use a small amount of spray adhesive to make the cheesecloth adhere to the cotton sheets.

3. Using spray laundry starch, lightly spray the inner layers of sheet cotton to help them stick together and conform to the shape of the leg.

Cotton-polyester quilt batting leg pads: You can purchase a large sheet of cotton-polyester quilt batting from a fabric store. Fold the sheet or cut it to size. It is about the same thickness as sheet cotton. Like sheet cotton, it does not hold up under washing, and it will last longer if covered with cheesecloth and sewn together or fastened with spray adhesive.

Polyester quilt-batting leg pads: This material is also available in large sheets from fabric stores. Unlike sheet cotton or cotton-polyester batting, it can be machine washed and dried. Because this material compresses a great deal, you must use extra layers to achieve the desired thickness. The layers may be stitched or secured together with quilt tacking or covered with cotton terry cloth.

DRESSING MATERIALS

Dressing materials are used to treat wounds. A dressing is applied over the wound and then held in place with a bandage. Wounds on the lower legs or joints require leg padding over the dressing; those on the heel or coronary band are usually held in place by a bandage without leg padding.

TYPES OF DRESSING MATERIALS

Non-stick sterile dressings: Available in rolls or in square pads; the 4-by-4-inch and 6-by-6-inch sizes are most useful. Applied to a wound after cleaning and medicating, they keep the wound clean, hold medication, and prevent exudate (serum and fluids) from the healing wound from sticking to the bandage.

Some dressings are made of sterile gauze pads or strips impregnated with petroleum jelly. These should not be used for first aid or applied to a wound that may have to be stitched.

U.S. Army sterile compress and bandage: Large sterile wound dressing made of cotton between a layer of paper and muslin, available from surplus stores and some tack shops. It is inexpensive, large, and thick enough to serve for a shipping bandage, but it cannot be washed or reused.

Disposable diapers: The large-size square type (without elastic edges) can be used for a variety of padding purposes. The plastic backing can be used to make a sweat bandage but must be removed for other bandages.

Terry-cloth towels: These make good padding for wet applications, cold-water bandages, or ice packs. They are durable, washable, and can be folded to fit.

Sanitary napkins: Thick, clean, and absorbent, they make an effective first-aid pad to stop bleeding and can be used as part of a pressure bandage.

FASTENERS

The end of a bandage must be securely fastened so that it cannot come loose and trip the horse. Fasteners must be placed on the outside of the leg, otherwise they can be pulled loose if struck by the opposite foot. They should be placed in the cannon area, never over a joint or on the back of a tendon. *A fastener must never be tighter than the bandage itself, so that it indents the bandage, and it must not be applied as a continuous ring around the leg.* This causes excessive pressure, which can interfere with circulation and lead to cording, or damage to the tendons.

Bandage pins: Large safety pins or diaper pins are sold in tack stores or drug stores. Use two pins per bandage, placed vertically, horizontally, or crossing each other. The pins must go through at least two layers of bandage, but not so many layers that they bunch up, won't close securely, or will stick the horse. Pins must always be placed on the outside of the leg.

Bandage pins.

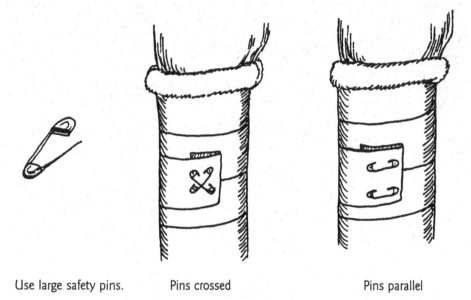

Use large safety pins.   Pins crossed   Pins parallel

Tape: Masking tape, adhesive tape, or plastic electrical tape may be used to fasten bandages or to reinforce other types of fastenings. Tape should be applied in several strips about a foot long, and *put on in a spiral—never in a continuous ring around the leg.* The tape should start on the opposite side of the leg from the end of the bandage.

Masking tape (and some other tapes) will not stick well in wet conditions and become useless if it has been frozen.

Velcro fasteners: Velcro is often sewn onto the end of bandages. It makes a good fastener if it is not applied in a continuous band which encircles the leg.

Velcro tends to pick up lint and debris, which makes it lose its holding power. Cleaning the hook and loop closures with a pin will help. A single-strip Velcro fastening should be reinforced with tape, pins, or sewing.

Sewn fastenings: Sewing is the safest way of securing the end of a bandage. Exercise bandages, which must be extra secure for jumping or fast work, are fastened by sewing the end of the bandage to the layers beneath it. Using heavy carpet thread and a curved needle, make simple stitches along the end of the wrap and for an inch or two along the sides.

Do not use the fabric ties that come attached to some bandages, because they create a tight ring of pressure around the horse's leg or tail, which may interfere with circulation and cause tendon or tissue damage. Fabric ties should be cut off.

Applying tape.

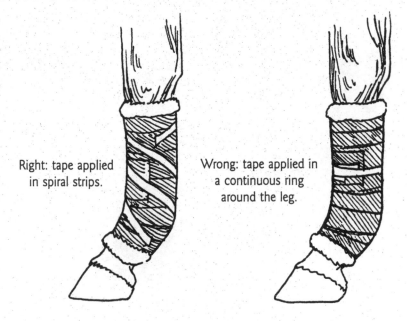

Right: tape applied
in spiral strips.

Wrong: tape applied in
a continuous ring
around the leg.

Sewn fastening.

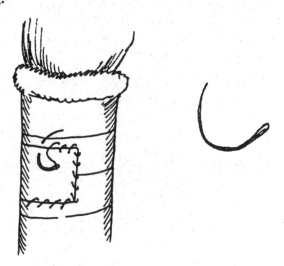

Stitch along end and sides of bandage.   Curved needle

BASIC BANDAGING TECHNIQUES

SAFETY WHEN BANDAGING

When bandaging, work in a safe, clear place with good lighting, preferably an aisle or grooming area rather than a stall. The horse should be safely tied, cross-tied, or held by an assistant—never loose in a stall.

Never sit or kneel close to a horse's legs; bend down or squat, but be sure you can get out of the way if the horse should move suddenly. If a horse is restless and picks up his leg while you are bandaging, an assistant can hold up his other front leg to keep him still.

It is best to wear your safety helmet when working around a horse's legs, in case he should kick or bump into you. Keep your head clear of the horse's legs; he might move restlessly or kick at a fly and hit you if you are in the way.

How to Bandage Safely and Correctly

- Before bandaging, assemble all wraps, leg padding, fasteners, and other materials you need. Wraps should be tightly rolled with Velcro fasteners on the inside.

- Stand the horse in a clean area, where the bandage will not get muddy or pick up bedding or debris. Placing a folded newspaper under the hoof will help keep the bandage clean (especially shipping bandages) if you don't have a clean surface to work on.

- Clean the horse's legs before bandaging, and make sure there is nothing underneath the padding that could rub, irritate the leg, or cause extra pressure. It is all right to bandage over a leg that is wet but clean; bandaging with an absorbent padding like sheet cotton is a good way to dry the leg.

- Make sure there is sufficient padding under the entire bandage and that the padding is smooth and distributed evenly so it will not put extra pressure on any part of the leg. Don't bandage over lumps, folds, or wrinkles.

- Start the padding on the outside of the leg, just behind the cannon bone, and wrap from front to back, outside to inside. (On the left legs, the padding and bandage should run counterclockwise; on the right legs, clockwise.) This is safer for the tendons.

- Always wrap the bandage in the same direction as the leg pad. This makes the inside of the bandage smoother and avoids creating a ridge that can press against the tendons and cause damage. Slip the end of the wrap under the edge of the leg pad and wrap once around to secure it. The best place to start is on the cannon bone, just above the fetlock joint.

- Wrap evenly, overlapping about one-third of the width of the bandage at each wrap. Put most of the pressure backward, against the front of the leg, instead of pulling forward, against the tendons. Check the bandage with your hand as you work, making sure that no wrap is tighter or looser than the rest.

- A bandage must not bind at the knee, hock, or fetlock joint. Don't bandage the back surface of the knee, as this can cause excessive pressure when the horse bends his knee. The padding must extend at least 1/2-inch beyond the top and bottom edges of the bandage to keep the edge of the bandage from binding.

- Fasten the bandage on the outside of the leg on the cannon area, never on a joint. If necessary, fold the extra end of the bandage under to make it end on the outside of the leg. The fastener should not make an indentation in the bandage. If reinforcing tape is used, apply strips in a spiral. Never apply a fastener or reinforcing tape in a continuous ring around the leg.

- A finished bandage should feel firm and even over its whole length. No part of the bandage should be looser or tighter, and you should be able to slip two fingers under the bandage.

- When you are learning to bandage, practice applying a bandage to a person's arm. He or she can tell you if the padding is smooth and if the wraps are too tight, too loose, or create uneven pressure.

Good bandaging practices.

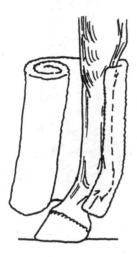

Place pad at back of cannon bone.

Place end of bandage under edge of leg pad. Wrap in same direction as leg pad.

Keep wraps even, overlapping by one-third width of bandage.

Finish on outside of leg. You should be able to slip two fingers inside the bandage.

Bandaging mistakes.

Lumpy, uneven bandage, insecurely pinned.

Inadequate padding. Fastened over a joint, with string ties in continuous ring around leg.

Tape applied in continuous ring, indenting bandage.

Pulling forward against tendon, indenting bandage.

REMOVING BANDAGES

When removing bandages, undo them gently but quickly by passing them in a ball from one hand to the other; don't try to roll them up as you take them off. Rub the horse's legs (especially the back tendons and fetlock joint) after removing the bandages. Re-roll the leg pads, and either re-roll the bandages for use again or set them aside to be laundered.

RUBBING LEGS

Rubbing legs is good therapy, as it helps to reduce swelling and stimulates the circulation. It is good for tired legs after hard work and to help stiff, arthritic joints and old, chronic injuries. Rubbing can also be used to dry wet legs, to help warm a chilled horse, and to refresh the legs after removing bandages.

Before rubbing a leg, you can apply a small amount of rubbing alcohol or a mild liniment or leg brace to lubricate your hands and make rubbing easier. Be careful to use a mild product that does not irritate the horse's skin and that is safe to bandage over, if you plan to wrap the leg.

Rubbing legs.

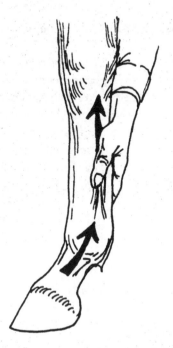

Grasp leg with fingers and rub upward, massaging fetlock joint and tendons.

Grasp the leg with your thumb and fingers and rub upward, toward the heart, with a gentle massaging motion. Work your fingers over the tendons, suspensory ligament, fetlock joint, and pastern. You must rub for at least 5 minutes per leg in order to do any good. When rubbing to dry a wet leg, use a dry terry-cloth towel or a handful of dry straw to absorb moisture and rub the leg dry.

CAUTION: Don't massage or apply liniment to a wound or a hot, painful swelling that might be caused by an infection. This could make the inflammation worse.

LINIMENTS AND LEG MEDICATIONS

If you use liniment or leg medication under bandages, make sure it is intended to be used under a bandage. Some horses are especially sensitive, and certain liniments may cause the skin to blister. The legs must be clean and dry when liniment or medication is applied; applying liniment to a wet leg and then wrapping it may cause blistering.

Rub a small amount of liniment into the leg, making sure that it has dried before bandaging over it. The liniment should be well rubbed in and the leg should be completely dry before you bandage it.

MAINTAINING BANDAGES

Stable or standing bandages should be removed and reset every 12 hours (usually morning and evening). Shipping bandages may be left on for up to 24 hours, but tail wraps should only be used for a few hours. Exercise bandages and polo wraps are for short-term use only and should be removed immediately after exercise. Some special-purpose bandages (especially those used to treat wounds) may be left in place longer; follow your veterinarian's instructions.

If a bandage has slipped, loosened, become wet or dirty, or if bedding or other material has worked its way underneath, it should be removed and replaced.

Always follow your veterinarian's instructions regarding any bandage he or she has applied or recommended. Ask how long the bandage should be left on, and whether you should change the bandage or if the veterinarian prefers to do it himself.

LAUNDERING, ROLLING, AND STORING BANDAGES

Bandages should be laundered when they are soiled. Stick Velcro fasteners together and place bandages in a mesh washing bag for machine washing, or wash them by hand. Use a mild detergent or 1 or 2 tablespoons of washing soda, and rinse thoroughly. Squeeze excess water out by hand instead of wringing them dry, to preserve the loft (fluffiness), and line dry. Bandages and cotton quilts are more likely to shrink if washed in hot water and machine dried.

When dry, bandages should be rolled ready for use. Roll bandages with Velcro closures on the inside. If you tuck the ends under the first layer of the roll, they will not unroll if dropped. Quilts, cottons, or leg pads should be stored rolled as they will be around the leg; this helps them conform better to the shape of the leg. Keep wraps and leg padding in a clean container so they do not pick up dirt, shavings, or other debris.

Rolling wraps and leg pads for reuse.

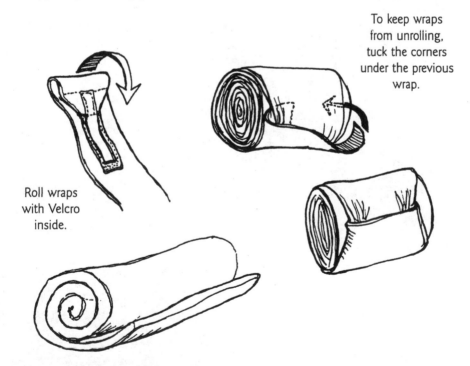

To keep wraps from unrolling, tuck the corners under the previous wrap.

Roll wraps with Velcro inside.

Leg pads rolled in direction in which they are used, to keep their shape.

SHIPPING, STABLE, AND TAIL BANDAGES

A shipping bandage protects the lower leg, coronary band, and the heels, in case a horse steps on his own feet, hits his legs, or scrambles during travel, loading, or unloading. It also offers some relief from road vibration and swelling. The bandage should extend from the ground (underneath the bulbs of the heels) to the base of the knee or hock, covering the pastern, fetlock joint, and tendons, and the padding must extend slightly above and below the edges of the bandage. A shipping bandage must be well padded and comfortably snug but not excessively tight (you should be able to slip two fingers under the bandage).

Shipping bandages must be fastened securely, as they can be clumsy and can trip a horse if they are applied too loosely and slip down. They must be fastened on the outside of the leg, so that the horse cannot pull the fastening loose if he should strike the inside of the leg with his opposite foot.

If you are not skilled enough to apply good shipping bandages, it is better to use shipping boots to protect your horse's legs during travel.

How to Apply a Shipping Bandage

What You Need

Four shipping-length leg wraps: Wraps can be cotton stockinette "track" bandages, knitted polyester wraps, or flannel bandages. They must be 12 to 16 feet long (depending on the size of the horse) in order to cover all parts of the leg and heel over the extra large leg pads.

Four shipping-length leg pads: These must be long enough to cover the leg from the base of the knee or hock to the ground. Leg pads for shipping bandages must be taller and thicker than those used for other types of bandages; most ready-made leg pads are too short. It is best to measure the horse's legs and make up leg pads to fit. For Pony Club purposes, sheet cotton is preferred for leg pads.

NEVER put on shipping bandages without leg pads!

Fasteners: Two bandage pins for each leg, plus masking tape.

PROCEDURE

1. With padding touching the ground, wrap it smoothly around the leg without wrinkles. Place the edge of the leg pad against the back of the cannon bone on the outside of the leg. Wrap from front to back and outside to inside.

2. Start the bandage near the middle of the cannon bone on the outside. Tuck the end under the edge of the padding and wrap once around the leg to anchor the bandage.

3. Wrap downward, overlapping each wrap about one third to one half of the width of the bandage, and keeping the wraps parallel each other. With each wrap, pull the bandage snug by pulling firmly backward against the cannon bone, rather than pulling forward against the tendons. Make the bandage firm enough to compress the padding evenly, but not so tight that you cannot get a finger underneath. Continue bandaging down over the ankle and pastern.

4. Make several turns around the bulbs of the heel and the coronary band. At least half the width of the bandage must go under the heel to keep the bandage from sliding up. (To make it easier to wrap under the heel, you can place the horse's foot on a board on the ground, with his heel extending backward off the board.) Be sure that the front of the bandage does not ride up above the coronary band.

5. Bandage back up the leg to just below the knee or hock. Leave at least a half inch of padding above the bandage, and make sure that it does not bind at the knee or hock when the horse moves his leg. Continue bandaging back down the leg.

6. Finish the bandage on the outside of the leg in the cannon area, not over a tendon or a joint. (You can fold the end of the bandage underneath itself for a few inches if necessary.) Fasten with bandage pins on the outside of the leg, and reinforce with strips of tape applied in a spiral.

Applying a shipping bandage.

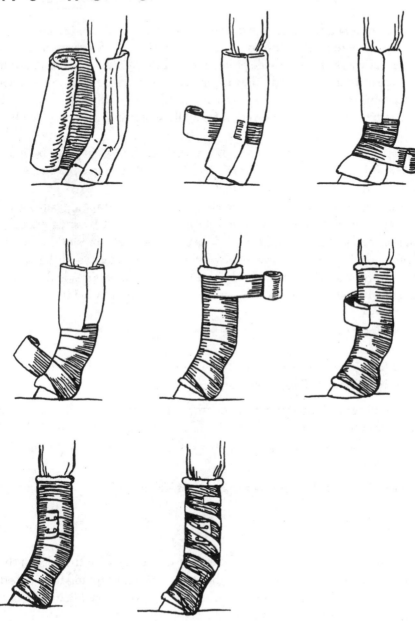

STABLE (STANDING) BANDAGES

Stable, or standing bandages have several purposes. They may be used to prevent "filling" or reduce swelling of the legs after hard work, for warmth, or to dry wet or muddy legs. They provide protection against injuries in the stall, and are used to treat injuries, to hold a dressing in place, or as a base over which a hock or knee bandage may be applied. When one leg is injured, the uninjured leg should also be bandaged, to prevent it from filling or swelling because the horse may put more weight on it.

When applying stable bandages, always bandage the legs in pairs: both front legs, both hind legs, or all four. Stable bandages must be removed and reset at least every 12 hours (morning and night).

A stable bandage is put on in much the same way as a shipping bandage, but it is shorter; it ends just below the fetlock joint. It must be snug enough to compress the padding around the tendons and other structures of the leg. The pressure must be evenly distributed over the entire bandage, and the bandage should not be too tight; you should be able to slip two fingers inside the finished bandage. The bandage must be run in the same direction as the leg pad.

What You Need

Two or four leg wraps: Flannel or knitted polyester or cotton stockinette bandages approximately 10 to 12 feet long.

Two or four leg pads: Sheet cottons or other leg pads sized to fit the horse's legs. They should reach from the lower edge of the knee or hock to just below the fetlock joint, cupping the ergot (usually 14 to 16 inches long, depending on the size of the horse).

Fasteners: Two bandage pins per leg, tape, or Velcro.

Procedure

1. Apply the leg pad starting on the outside of the leg, with the edge of the pad in the groove at the back of the cannon bone, wrapping from outside to inside. The padding should reach from the base of the knee or hock to below the fetlock joint, cupping the ergot.

2. Start the bandage on the outside of the cannon bone, tucking the end under the edge of the pad. Take one wrap to anchor the bandage, then wrap downward to the fetlock joint.

3. At the fetlock joint, drop the wrap under the back of the joint, cupping the ergot, and bring it up higher in front. This makes an upside down "vee" at the front of the joint, which creates a sling support for the fetlock joint and allows the leg to bend. Leave a half inch of padding below the bandage, to keep the edge of the bandage from binding.

Applying a stable bandage.

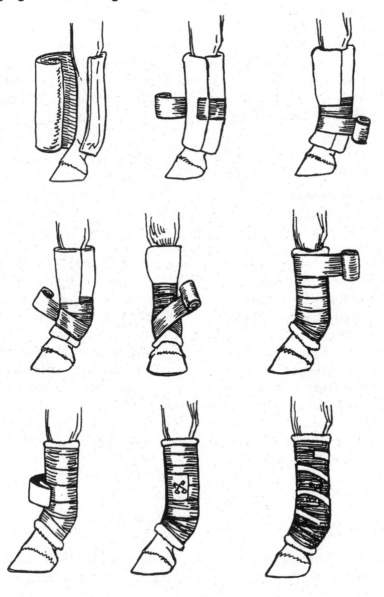

4. Wrap back up the leg, to just below the knee. Leave a half inch of pad-ding above the edge of the bandage, to keep the bandage from binding the knee or tendons. Wrap back downward, but don't use excessive pressure over the previous wraps.

5. Finish the bandage on the outside of the leg, in the cannon area, never over a tendon or joint. Fold the end back under for a few inches if necessary. Fasten with the bandage's Velcro closure, bandage pins and/or tape applied in a spiral.

When a stable bandage is used to hold a wound dressing in place, the wound should first be cleaned and treated, and a dressing applied. The dressing is held in place by wrapping lightly with conforming gauze, then the stable bandage is applied over it. The leg pad and bandage should be applied in the direction that best supports closure of the wound.

TAIL BANDAGES

A tail bandage is used to protect the hair of the dock during shipping, to contain the tail hairs during breeding, foaling, or body clipping, or to shape the hair of the dock during grooming. A tail wrap can be also be used to keep the skirt of the tail clean, or to protect a braided tail before a show.

Tail wraps may be cotton stockinette or polyester knit bandages, or synthetic crepe bandages (such as VetRap). Elastic bandages (Ace® bandages) may also be used, but with caution, as they can easily be applied tightly enough to impair circulation and cause tissue damage. An old elastic bandage which has lost most of its elasticity through use and washing is safer for tail bandaging.

Tail wraps should be fastened with Velcro, pins, or tape applied in spiral strips. Do not use fabric tapes or string ties, found on some older types of bandages, or any type of fastener which creates a continuous ring of pressure around the dock. These can impair the circulation and cause serious damage to the dock.

CAUTION: Tail bandages must be used carefully to avoid damage to the tail. They should only be applied for an hour or so, or for shipping, for a few hours. A tail wrap that is put on too tightly, fastened incorrectly, or left in place too long can impair the circulation, causing discomfort, swelling, loss of hair, and even gangrene, which could require amputation of the tail.

SHIPPING TAIL BANDAGE

For shipping purposes, a tail bandage should protect the hair of the dock from being rubbed against the back of the trailer. It must be put on securely so it will not slip but must never be wrapped too tightly or left on for more than a few hours. When traveling for more than a few hours or for long distance shipping by a commercial carrier, a tail guard made of leather or synthetic material should be used instead of a tail bandage.

WHAT YOU NEED

Tail bandage: 4-inch-wide bandage in a slightly stretchy material, such as cotton stockinette or polyester knit track bandage.

Fastener: Velcro fastener, pins, or tape applied in spiral strips. Do not use fabric tape or string fasteners, or any fastener which creates a continuous ring of pressure around the dock.

PROCEDURE

1. Start the wrap about 4 inches below the top of the tail. Lay the end of the bandage on top of the tail, and make one complete turn to secure it.

2. The following are methods to prevent a tail wrap from slipping down:

    *   *Turning up locks of hair:* Wrap upward, to the top of the tail, then continue down for 8 to 10 inches. Pull out a small section of hair (pointing upward), and take one wrap over it. Fold the end of the hair downward, and continue wrapping over it. Wrapping a small section of hair into the bandage like this anchors the bandage and keeps it from slipping down. This should be repeated once or twice farther down the bandage.

    *   *Herringbone bandage:* After the first two or three wraps, wrap diagonally down and across the front of the tail, then bring the next wrap diagonally up and across. Alternate diagonal wraps, down to the end of the tail. This creates a herringbone pattern, which makes the bandage less likely to slip down.

    *   *Butterfly bandage:* Wrap for several turns, then give the bandage a half twist as it crosses the front of the tail. Wrap for several turns (the bandage will be inside out), then make another half twist. If you make a half twist every three or four turns, the bandage will show a series of vees or "butterflies." The twists help to prevent slipping.

4. Wrap to the end of the dock, then back upward until you reach the end of the bandage. Fasten the bandage on the outside of the tail with a Velcro fastener, pins, or tape applied in spiral strips. *Never wrap a continuous band of tape around the tail.*

5. To keep the skirt of the tail clean and free from tangles during shipping:

    - Wrap its entire length (this may require a second bandage or an extra long bandage).

    - Pull a nylon stocking (or one leg cut from a pair of pantyhose) or a ready-made fabric tail bag over the skirt and pin it to the tail bandage.

    - Braid the skirt of the tail into a single braid, fold it up on top of the bandaged dock, and cover it with a second tail wrap.

Shipping tail bandage.

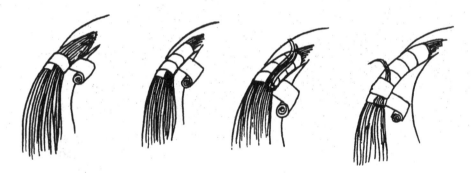

Turning up locks of hair to anchor bandage.

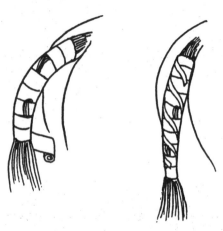

Finished bandage, fastened with tape.

Shipping tail bandage, alternate methods.

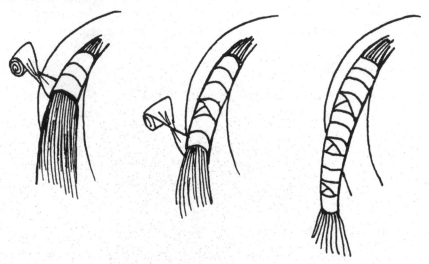

Butterfly wrap   Make a half twist every three or four wraps.

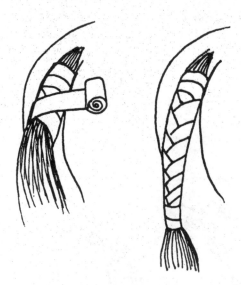

Herringbone wrap.   Alternate diagonal upward and downward wraps.

GROOMING TAIL BANDAGE

A tail wrap may be used to smooth and lay down the top hairs of the dock before a competition or formal presentation. It only needs to be in place for half an hour or so to achieve the desired result.

A braided tail should be protected with a tail wrap when the horse is not showing. Braided tails should not be left in overnight, whether wrapped or not; the braided hairs will break off, spoiling the appearance of the tail.

WHAT YOU NEED

Tail bandage: A stretchy bandage such as a cotton or polyester knitted track bandage, elastic crepe bandage, or 4-inch elastic (Ace) bandage.

CAUTION: *An elastic bandage should only be left on for half an hour.*

Fastener: Velcro closure (on bandage), pins, or strips of tape.

PROCEDURE

1. Dampen the tail hair slightly.

   CAUTION: Do not wet the bandage, as it may shrink and damage the tail.

2. Start the bandage close to the top of the tail. Wrap around once to secure end of bandage, then wrap up to the very top of the tail.

3. Wrap downward to the end of the dock, then upward to end of bandage.

4. Fasten with Velcro closure, pins, or spiral strips of tape, but not tightly enough to cause an indentation, and not in a continuous ring. When an elastic bandage is applied only for a short time, it can be fastened by tucking the end inside one of the wraps.

Grooming tail bandage.

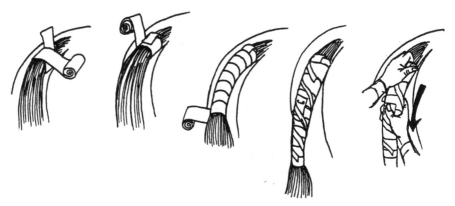

To remove the bandage from an unbraided tail, grasp the bandage firmly with the fingers hooked over the top of the bandage on both sides, and pull straight down. For a braided tail, unwrap the bandage.

TAIL-COVERING BANDAGE

This bandage is used to temporarily contain the hair of the entire tail, to keep it out of the way during body clipping, or to prevent contamination during breeding or foaling. It is only intended to be left on for a short time.

WHAT YOU NEED

Tail bandage: An elastic crepe bandage (VetRap) works best, or cotton stockinette or knit track bandage. If the tail is long and thick, an extra long bandage or a second bandage may be necessary.

Fastener: Velcro closure (on bandage), pins, or tape (in strips).

Rubber band: To fasten braid.

PROCEDURE

1. Braid the skirt of the tail into a long single braid, and fold it up over the dock.

2. Start the tail wrap as usual, a few inches from the top of the dock. Apply a tail bandage over the braid and dock, covering the entire tail.

3. Fasten with Velcro, pins, or tape strips.

Tail-covering bandage.

EXERCISE BANDAGES AND POLO WRAPS

EXERCISE BANDAGES

Exercise bandages protect the lower legs, especially the flexor tendons and suspensory ligaments, during work. They are used when horses are likely to strike themselves or require extra protection, especially during longeing, lateral work, galloping, jumping, or polo, and on young horses or horses recovering from a leg injury. It was previously thought that exercise bandages supported the flexor tendons and suspensory ligaments, but most experts now believe that they offer protection rather than significant support.

Exercise wraps extend from just below the knee or hock joint to the fetlock joint. Care must be taken not to restrict the movement of the fetlock joint. Exercise bandages are always applied in pairs (that is, both front legs, both hind legs, or all four legs).

CAUTION: *Exercise bandages must be applied correctly or they may do great harm.* They are applied over parts of the leg which are vulnerable to injury, and are used during demanding athletic work. An improperly applied bandage can restrict movement of the fetlock joint, interfere with circulation, and damage or even bow a tendon. A loose or incorrectly fastened bandage can slip down or come undone and cause a serious stumble.

To learn to apply exercise bandages, you must have hands-on instruction from an expert. If your horse requires lower leg protection and you are not experienced enough to put exercise bandages on correctly, it is safer to use protective boots such as sport-medicine boots or galloping boots.

WHAT YOU NEED

Leg wraps: Elastic crepe bandage (VetRap or other brand) is preferred. Saratoga bandages are preferable for use in wet conditions because they do not absorb water. Cotton or polyester stockinette track bandages are less satisfactory, as they have less stretch and tend to become heavy and loosen when wet.

Leg pads: Sheet cottons folded or cut to fit, or Kendall cottons. Leg padding is thinner than that used in stable bandages, but must be thick enough to compress and to distribute the pressure of the wraps. Padding must be wrinkle free, as wrinkles cause areas of uneven pressure.

Fasteners: Safety pins and/or needle and thread. Velcro fasteners alone are not secure enough for exercise bandages and should be reinforced with pins or sewing. Safety pins may be used for ordinary work, but for fast work, the end of the bandage must be sewn down for extra security (see below).

PROCEDURE

1. Start a half inch from the top, on the outside of the leg, with the end of the wrap tucked inside the edge of the leg pad. Wrap from front to back and outside to inside.

2. Wrap down the leg, keeping each wrap horizontal and parallel to the last wrap, and overlapping each wrap by about half the width of the bandage. When wrapping, pull backward against the shin, not forward against the tendon, and keep the tension even.

3. At the fetlock joint, drop one-half width of wrap down under the back of the joint, bringing it up to the top of the fetlock joint in front to form an upside down "vee." This protects the fetlock joint and the suspensory ligament, while still allowing free movement of the joint.

4. Wrap back up the leg, taking care not to wrap too tightly. Finish the bandage on the outside of the leg, at the middle of the cannon bone. If necessary, fold any excess bandage underneath itself.

5. Fasten the bandage securely, using one of the following methods:

   - Two safety pins, applied through several layers of bandage and padding. (Pins must be reinforced by sewing.)

   - Sewn fastening: using a large needle and carpet thread, sew the end of the bandage to the wraps underneath. (A curved needle is easiest to use.)

Applying an exercise bandage.

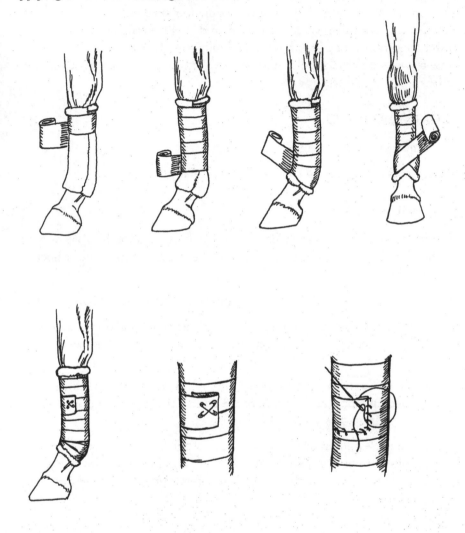

POLO WRAPS

Polo wraps or Sandown bandages are fleece bandages that are designed to be used without padding underneath. They are slightly stretchy, conform easily to the shape of the leg, and are quick and easy to apply. They are often used in place of exercise bandages for light leg protection during longeing, schooling, turnout, and ring work.

Polo wraps are not recommended for jumping or cross-country work because they are neither as secure nor as protective as correctly applied exercise bandages, sport-medicine boots, or galloping boots. Because they are used without padding underneath, they can easily apply too much or uneven pressure to the tendons, causing impaired circulation and possible tendon damage. If used in wet conditions, they absorb water and may stretch, slip, or come loose. Because of these drawbacks, polo wraps are not permitted in U.S. Pony Club competitions or rating tests.

WHAT YOU NEED

Polo bandages: Usually used on all four legs.

Fasteners: Pins or masking tape, to reinforce Velcro fasteners.

PROCEDURE

1. Unroll 8 to 10 inches of bandage. Starting at the back of the knee or hock, hold the bandage end diagonally across the outside of the knee or hock, with the end toward the front of the horse.

2. Take one turn around the leg, over the base of the diagonal bandage end.

3. Fold the bandage end downward, over the first wrap and down the back of the flexor tendons. This cushions the tendons and keeps the bandage from slipping.

4. Wrap downward, over the bandage end, keeping each wrap parallel to the last, overlapping half the width of the bandage and keeping the tension even.

5. At the fetlock joint, drop half the width of the bandage down underneath the joint, bringing it up in front to form an upside-down "vee." It should not be loose, but must not be tight enough to restrict movement of the fetlock joint.

6. Wrap upward and finish the bandage on the outside of the cannon bone (not on the tendon, shin or fetlock joint). Most polo wraps have Velcro closures. These should be reinforced with pins or spiral tape.

Applying a polo wrap.

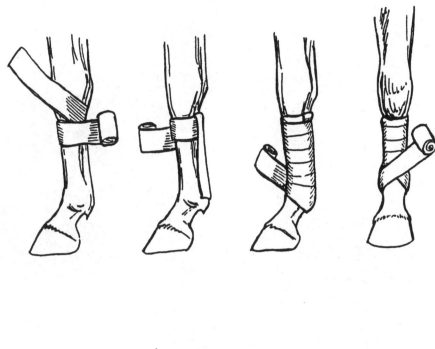

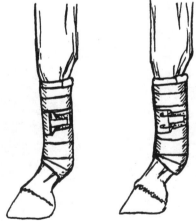

TREATMENT AND SPECIAL PURPOSE BANDAGES

Treatment bandages are used to treat and protect wounds, sprains, strains, and other injuries, or to prevent swelling caused by a recent injury.

Treatment bandages may be left in place for varying periods, depending on their purpose. Wound dressings are usually not removed more often than once a day, to avoid disturbing the healing surface too often. Ice packs and cold water bandages are usually used for relatively short periods (20 minutes to several hours), while a sweat or a poultice may be left on for 12 hours or so.

Follow your veterinarian's instructions on how often to change treatment bandages.

CAUTION: The following are special-purpose bandages, which must be applied by an experienced person, along with the proper course of treatment.

STABLE BANDAGE WITH WOUND DRESSING

When bandaging a wound, the wound should first be cleaned and treated, and a non-stick dressing applied. The leg pad and bandage should be applied in the direction that best supports closure of the wound.

When applying a dressing and stable bandage as first aid, the wound should be cleaned but not medicated. This is especially important if it may need to be stitched.

PRESSURE BANDAGE

A pressure bandage may be used to stop bleeding, to prevent swelling caused by a recent injury, or to inhibit the formation of proud flesh. It is applied firmly, with enough padding to create a uniform counter-pressure which prevents swelling or stops bleeding. It should be wrapped in the direction that best supports closure of the wound.

WHAT YOU NEED

Depending on the kind of wound and the purpose of the pressure bandage, any of the following materials may be used:

Dressing or pressure pad: Sterile non-stick gauze pads are best; sanitary napkins are good for stopping bleeding.

Leg padding: Sheet cotton or equivalent, folded to fit.

Wraps: Elastic adhesive tape (Elastikon, Elastoplast), VetRap (preferred for bandaging heel grabs), Ace bandage, or knit stockinette "track" bandage.

Fasteners: Safety pins and/or strips of masking tape.

PROCEDURE

1. To stop bleeding, a pressure bandage must be applied quickly and proficiently. The wound should usually be cleaned first, but if bleeding is serious, skip this step and apply pressure at once. Place a clean pad (sterile gauze pad or sanitary napkin, if available) over the wound and apply elastic adhesive tape or VetRap directly over the pad, using firm, even pressure. If blood soaks through the pad and bandage, do not remove the first pad, but add more padding over it. Removing the pad may cause bleeding to start again; this should be left to the veterinarian. This type of pressure bandage should not be left in place for more than a few hours, and must not cut off circulation.

2. To hold the edges of a cut together or to inhibit the growth of proud flesh, use a sterile gauze dressing covered by a few layers of padding, then two pieces of sheet cotton. Wrap with elastic adhesive tape or VetRap, in the direction that best supports closure of the wound.

3. To treat a heel grab (overreach injury), clean the wound and apply nitrofurazone or another mild topical ointment. Cover with a sterile gauze dressing, then wrap the heel, coronary band, and foot with elastic adhesive tape or VetRap. Wrap tightly enough to hold the edges of the wound

together so it can heal. The bottom part of the wrap (on the hoof) can be protected with duct tape, but do not use duct tape above the coronary band.

Pressure bandage.

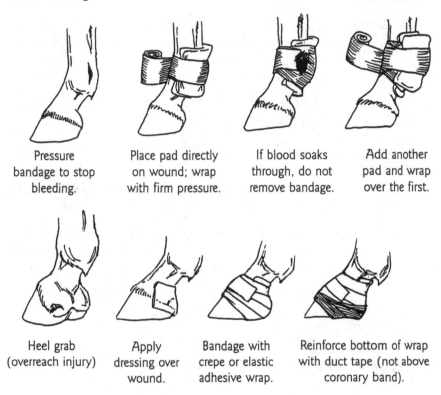

Pressure bandage to stop bleeding.	Place pad directly on wound; wrap with firm pressure.	If blood soaks through, do not remove bandage.	Add another pad and wrap over the first.
Heel grab (overreach injury)	Apply dressing over wound.	Bandage with crepe or elastic adhesive wrap.	Reinforce bottom of wrap with duct tape (not above coronary band).

ICE PACKS

An ice pack is used to reduce pain, heat, and swelling due to a recent injury, especially sprains, strains, and bruises. For best effect, ice packs should be applied to the injury as soon as possible and left on for 20 to 30 minutes at a time, repeating as often as necessary. Cold applications are most effective immediately after an injury and for the first 48 hours.

WHAT YOU NEED

Two elastic (Ace) bandages: 6 inches wide.

Padding: Terry-cloth towels are most effective.

Two plastic bags: (food storage size), with zip-like closures or freezer tape.

Cooling packs: Ice or gel.

Fastener: Safety pins work best.

PROCEDURE

1. Double bag the plastic bags; fill with chopped ice, and tape them shut. Gel cooling packs must be placed in the freezer to cool them before use. A package of frozen peas or corn makes a convenient ice pack which conforms easily to the shape of the leg.

2. Apply the ice pack or gel pack to the injury, and wrap with several layers of terry cloth towel for insulation as well as padding.

3. Wrap an Ace bandage firmly over the ice and towels, and fasten on the outside with safety pins.

4. When the ice begins to melt, apply the second Ace bandage over the first to keep the whole application from sagging away from the injury site.

5. When using an ice pack, the skin at the back of the pastern should be covered with petroleum jelly, to prevent chapping from exposure to cold and wet. This is not necessary when using a gel pack.

6. Remove the entire wrap as soon as the ice is melted, or it will become a sweat wrap, producing heat instead of cold. Apply fresh ice packs as often as necessary.

Applying an ice pack.

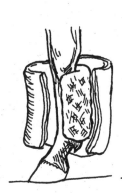   

| Apply petroleum jelly to heels and pastern. Apply ice pack and pad with folded towel. | Wrap with 6-inch Ace bandage. | Wrap with firm, even pressure. | When wrap begins to sag, apply a second Ace bandage over the first. |

COLD-WATER BANDAGES

Cold-water bandages are used to apply cold and pressure to a leg for several hours. They can be used as first aid after a sprain or strain, or to reduce pain, heat, and swelling. They are most effective when applied after cold-hosing (see USPC *Manual of Horsemanship* [Book 2], page 232.)

Cold-water bandages must be kept wet. If allowed to dry, they may shrink and cause excessive or uneven pressure, compounding the injury. For this reason, they cannot be left on overnight.

WHAT YOU NEED

Knit stockinette "track" wrap.

Padding: Should be durable when wet (preferably a cotton quilted pad or terry-cloth towels).

Fasteners: Safety pins are best. Do not use tape.

Bucket of ice water.

Petroleum jelly (Vaseline®).

PROCEDURE

1. Apply petroleum jelly to the skin of the heels and pastern, to protect against chapping.

2. Soak the padding in ice water until it is thoroughly wet and cold.

3. Without wringing it out, apply the padding to the leg. Bandage snugly, as pressure is part of the purpose of this wrap.

4. Frequently run cold water over the entire wrap, especially between the leg and the padding. Keep the entire bandage wet.

POULTICE

A poultice is a "drawing" medication that draws infection or inflammation from wounds such as puncture wounds, or reduces the inflammation (pain, heat, and swelling) that accompanies a sprain or bruise. Poultices are sometimes used on tendons as a precautionary measure to prevent swelling or "filling" after hard work. A hot poultice is used to increase circulation; a cold one is used to decrease heat and inflammation.

WHAT YOU NEED

Bandage and leg padding: Of a type suitable for the area to be poulticed.

6-by-6-inch gauze pad (unfolded), or gauze material.

Brown paper bag or newspaper.

Plastic food wrap.

Nylon stocking or one leg cut from a pair of pantyhose.

Poultice material: Such as Antiphlogistine® or poultice powder.

Spatula: For applying poultice.

PROCEDURE

1. Prepare the poultice according to manufacturer's directions. For a hot poultice, mix poultice powder with warm water and heat in a double boiler, or place poultice on brown paper and heat in a microwave oven. The poultice must be warm, not hot, as it will hold heat for a considerable length of time and can burn the leg if it is too hot.

2. Cut paper to the size of the padding. Apply the poultice to the paper with a spatula or with your hands, and form it to the size and shape of the area to be covered, 1/4 inch thick. Wetting your hands makes it easier to spread the poultice without it sticking to you. To make removal easier, cover the poultice with gauze material.

3. Clean the horse's leg, and place the nylon stocking over the foot. Then apply the entire pack (gauze side to the horse) to the area to be poulticed. Cover with plastic wrap to keep in the moisture and heat. Pull up the nylon hose, which will help keep the poultice in place as you bandage.

4. Place padding over the wrap and bandage.

5. Leave on for 12 to 24 hours. When the poultice is removed, any remaining poultice material should be washed off the leg with soap and water.

Applying a poultice.

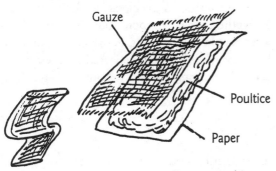

Gauze

Poultice

Paper

Cut nylon stocking
or pantyhose.

Prepare poultice.
Pull hose over foot.

Apply poultice to leg,
paper side out. Cover with
plastic wrap.

Pull hose up over poultice
to hold it in place.

Apply a stable bandage
over poultice.

Sweat Bandage

A sweat bandage is used to reduce swelling by increasing blood circulation through heat. Sweats are usually used for swellings that are more than 48 hours old; a fresh injury usually benefits more from cold applications. A sweat is left on for 8 hours (usually overnight) and then removed. It can be repeated if necessary.

Sweats should not be applied over liniments, blistering agents, or leg paints, or they may cause blistering of the skin.

What You Need

Sweat medication: Nitrofurazone ointment, or other sweat medication approved by your veterinarian.

Plastic food wrap: Or brown paper bag, newspaper, or disposable diaper with the plastic liner left intact.

Bandage and leg padding: Should be suitable for area to be sweated.

Procedure

1. Wash the leg and allow it to dry.

2. Apply Nitrofurazone ointment or sweat medication, rubbing it in as directed.

3. Cover the area lightly with plastic wrap, newspaper, brown paper, or disposable diaper with plastic toward the horse; do not pull it tight.

4. Place padding over the leg, and bandage.

Bandaging the Knee and Hock

Bandaging joints such as the knee and hock presents special problems. It is more difficult to achieve uniform pressure, and a bandage must not bind or apply excessive pressure to bony prominences like the back of the knee or the point of the hock, or to the tendons in this area. In some cases, the purpose of the bandage is to restrict or prevent movement of the joint; in others, the bandage must remain in place without slipping even though there will be some movement.

A stable bandage should be applied to the lower leg first. This serves as a base for the knee or hock bandage, to keep it from slipping down, and also prevents swelling of the lower leg.

Applying a sweat bandage.

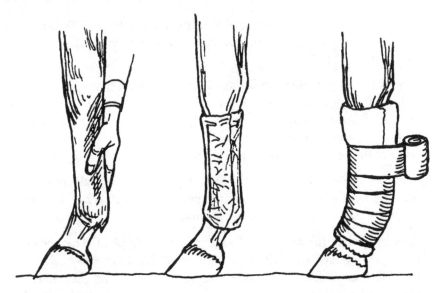

Apply sweat medication.   Cover with plastic wrap.   Apply a stable bandage
over the plastic wrap.

There are two main types of knee and hock bandages:

Spider (Many-Tailed) Bandage

A spider bandage is used to protect thick wraps covering a joint. It permits some movement in the joint and is preferred for the first 24 to 48 hours after an injury, as it is less likely to create pressure points than a figure-eight bandage.

What You Need

Spider bandage: Made from a large piece of fabric such as bandage flannel, a tee shirt, or blanket material. It should measure 24 by 30 inches. The two ends are cut into 10-inch strips roughly 1¹/₂ inches wide, leaving a 10- to 12-inch section in the middle.

Padding: To protect bony prominences on the knee or hock; terry-cloth towels or sheet cotton works well. Padding must be thick enough to compress evenly into the hollows of the joint and should be cut or folded to fit.

Wound dressings and medications: If needed.

Leg pad and wrap: For stable bandage, to be applied below the spider bandage.

PROCEDURE

1. Apply a stable bandage to the leg below the knee or hock. This keeps the spider bandage in place and helps to prevent swelling of the leg below the joint.

2. Apply dressing and medication as needed, then cover the joint with padding (terry-cloth towels or sheet cotton) which extends from mid-cannon to mid-forearm or mid-gaskin. There must be enough padding to prevent pressure damage to the Achilles tendon above the hock, the point of the hock, or the bony prominence at the back of the knee.

3. Place the spider bandage over the joint with the middle of the bandage over the front of the knee, or over the back of the hock. The "tails" or strips will be tied on the outside of the joint.

4. Start by tying at the middle, to hold the bandage in place. Then begin at the top, tying each set of ties in a square knot. Tuck the ends of the previous knot under the next one, to eliminate loose ends. Another method is to braid the ties, using a French braid as in braiding a tail. This method conforms better to the leg as it moves and is less likely to cause pressure points than knots. (see diagram).

FIGURE-EIGHT BANDAGE

A figure-eight bandage is used to wrap the knee or hock. It limits movement in the joint. Care must be taken to avoid pressure on bony prominences at the back of the knee and the point of the hock, and to keep the pressure even.

WHAT YOU NEED

Wrap and padding: For stable bandage, to be applied on the lower leg below the figure-eight bandage.

Padding: For knee or hock; terry-cloth towels or sheet cottons. Padding must be long enough to extend from halfway down the cannon to well above the joint, part way up the forearm or gaskin.

Several long bandages: Knit stockinette "track" bandages or elastic crepe bandage rolls (VetRap or other brand).

Dressing and/or medication: As needed.

Fastener: Safety pins.

Two rolls of gauze or two large sanitary pads: For hock bandage, for additional padding below the Achilles tendon.

Applying a spider bandage.

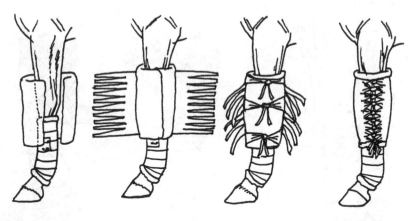

Place pad over stable bandage.

Place spider bandage over pad.

Tie top, middle (first), and bottom ties.

Finished spider bandage with ties fastened.

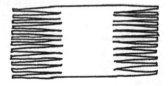

Spider bandage.

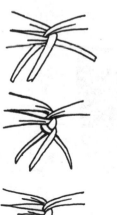

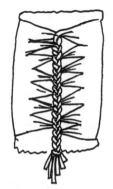

Fastening ties by braiding.

Figure-eight wrap for the knee.

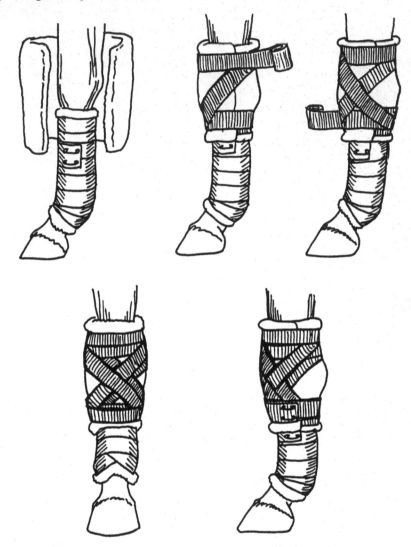

Procedure for the Knee

1. Put on a stable bandage to prevent swelling of the lower leg and to keep the figure-eight bandage from slipping down.

2. Apply wound dressing and/or medication, as indicated.

3. Place padding around the knee, from mid-cannon to mid-forearm.

4. Begin wrapping at the bottom of the padding. Tuck the end of the bandage under the edge of the padding and wrap once or twice to secure it.

5. Pass the wrap diagonally upward, wrap once around the top of the padding, then wrap diagonally downward. This forms a figure eight, crossing in front. The diagonal wraps should alternate to the outside and inside. Never wrap over the bony prominence at the back of the knee.

6. Continue to alternate wrapping around the bottom of the knee, diagonally upward, around the top, and diagonally downward, until you reach the end of the bandage. If necessary, continue with a second bandage over the end of the first, until the joint is wrapped. Finish the bandage on the outside, at the bottom of the knee wrap.

PROCEDURE FOR THE HOCK

1. Apply a stable bandage to the lower leg below the hock.

2. Place padding over the hock joint.

3. Start the hock wrap at the bottom of the padding, tucking the end under the edge of the padding and wrapping once or twice around.

4. Pass the bandage diagonally upward, across the side of the hock.

   When making the first wrap around above the hock, place two rolled bandages or thick sanitary pads in the hollows on each side below the Achilles' tendon. This helps to prevent excessive pressure directly on the tendon.

5. Take one complete wrap around the gaskin, then bring the wrap diagonally downward, across the front of the hock, and wrap around the base of the hock. This forms a figure eight, with the crossover point on the front of the hock, allowing the joint some movement. The diagonal wraps should alternate to the outside and inside. Never wrap over the point of the hock.

6. Repeat this process (diagonally upward, around the top, diagonally downward, and around the bottom) until you reach the end of the bandage. Use a second bandage if necessary.

7. Finish the bandage at the bottom of the wrap, on the outside, and fasten with pins.

Figure-eight bandage for the hock.

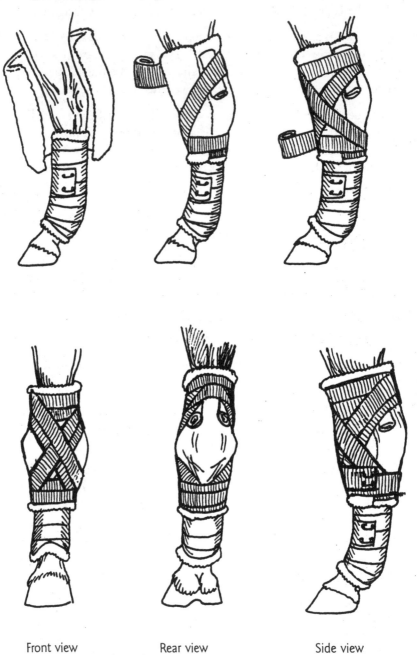

Front view   Rear view   Side view

Immobilizing Bandages

An immobilizing bandage is used to prevent movement of a joint. Immobilizing bandages, sometimes with splinting materials, are used when a fracture is suspected, to prevent movement which can worsen the injury. Because it can make the injury worse or damage the joint if incorrectly applied, an immobilizing bandage must be put on by an expert, and only under a veterinarian's direct supervision.

Splinting materials should only be applied by a veterinarian, because of the danger of aggravating the injury through uneven pressure or puncturing the joint if the splint material should break.

Because immobilizing bandages must be applied only under direct veterinary supervision, the procedure is not described here. However, you should have materials for such bandages on hand in case of emergency.

What You Need

Leg wrap and padding: For stable bandage, which is applied to the lower leg first.

Many layers of padding material: Large bed pillows or terry-cloth towels work well.

Bandages: Several track bandages, Ace bandages, or a spider bandage.

Fasteners: Safety pins, tape to reinforce bandage.

BOOTS AND THEIR USE

There are many kinds of boots on the market to protect the horse's feet and legs during work, turnout, and travel. Boots are often a good alternative to bandages because they are quick and easy to put on, offer good protection against injury, and are less likely to cause damage to legs than improperly applied bandages.

BOOT MATERIALS

Leather: Leather boots are sturdy and provide good protection against blows. However, the leather may stiffen and deteriorate with exposure to sweat, mud, and water, and may then irritate the skin. Leather boots should be cleaned with saddle soap after each use.

Rubber: Rubber boots are flexible and waterproof. Bell boots are often made of rubber, and rubber padding is sometimes used as a liner or as extra padding over the spot the boots are designed to protect. Rubber causes the legs to sweat, which may lead to skin irritation, especially in hot weather.

Plastic, vinyl, or PVC: Tough, light, flexible, and waterproof; often used for bell boots and molded splint boots. They may incorporate foam padding for extra protection. Plastics do not "breathe" or absorb moisture, so they will cause sweating.

Fabric: Boots may be made of felt, nylon felt, or other materials. Some boots are covered with a special fabric which allows Velcro strap closures to adhere to it. Felt or fleece may also be used as a lining, which makes a boot fit more comfortably and reduces its tendency to cause sweating and abrasions.

Fastenings: Boots may be fastened with leather straps with buckles, elastic straps with clips, Velcro strips, or other closures. Double Velcro closures (in which a second strip covers the first fastening) are much more secure than single Velcro strips. Velcro loses its ability to grip when it becomes clogged with dirt or debris.

TYPES OF BOOTS

SHIPPING BOOTS

Shipping boots are used to protect the legs during travel. These are a good choice if you are not skilled enough to apply shipping bandages properly. Like shipping bandages, they should protect the leg from the ground to the knee or hock. Some models are designed to also protect the front of the knees and the back of the hocks. They usually fasten with Velcro closures.

Shipping boots made of a "breathable" material are preferable to those made of plastic or foam rubber, which will cause sweating and may irritate the horse's legs, especially in hot weather.

Be sure to measure your horse's legs and buy shipping boots that are long enough. Many models are too short to cover the whole leg and the coronary band.

Shipping boots.

Fetlock or Ankle Boots

These are used on horses that interfere (strike the fetlock joint with the opposite foot), usually on the hind legs. If the horse only strikes one leg, a single boot can be used.

Ankle boots: Usually made of leather, with buckles on the outside and a pad over the inside of the fetlock joint.

Folded felt (Yorkshire) boots: The boot is unfolded and fastened around the leg (usually with Velcro; do not use the type equipped with fabric ties, as these can cord the tendons). The top portion is then folded down over the fetlock joint.

Rubber pastern rings: A rubber ring, buckled around the pastern to prevent interfering at this point.

Splint Boots (Brushing Boots)

Splint boots are designed to protect the leg from accidental blows, especially on the inside of the splint and cannon bones. They are made of leather, rubber, plastic, or fabric, with extra padding on the inside. They are often used for longeing, lateral work, or on young horses that may knock themselves and are vulnerable to splints.

Galloping Boots (Tendon Boots)

Galloping boots protect the entire lower leg, including the tendons, shins, and fetlock joint, from blows and high overreach injuries when galloping and jumping. They are often made of leather and fasten with elastic and leather straps.

Open-Front Boots

Open-front boots are used on show jumpers. They protect the back and sides of the lower leg but leave the shin exposed so that the horse feels it if he carelessly rubs a rail.

Sport-Medicine Boots

Sport-medicine boots are a recent innovation. They are made of sturdy, shock-absorbing synthetic material, with Velcro fasteners and a fetlock sling strap which helps to prevent overextension of the fetlock joint. Scientific studies have shown that sport-medicine boots absorb some energy, which may help to reduce the effects of concussion. They also offer good protection against blows or interfering.

Sport-medicine boots are often used during schooling, longeing, turnout, and strenuous work, and when bringing a horse back to fitness after a leg injury. Because they are easier to put on than exercise wraps and are less likely to cause damage to the tendons, sport-medicine boots are a good choice for horse owners who are not skilled enough to apply exercise bandages correctly.

BELL BOOTS (OVERREACH BOOTS)

Bell boots protect the heels against heel grabs and overreach injuries, and may help to keep front shoes from being torn off by the hind feet. They are especially necessary when jumping or galloping in mud, on horses that play violently during turnout, and on horses that are prone to forge or overreach.

Bell boots come in two different styles:

Closed: Most secure, but harder to put on and take off. Turn them inside out to pull them over the hoof, then turn them down once in place. They go on more easily if warmed in hot water first.

Open: Split boots which close with a buckle, plastic closure, or Velcro closure. Double Velcro closures are more secure.

PUTTING ON BOOTS

Both the boots and the horse's legs should be clean and dry when putting on boots. Place the boot slightly higher on the leg, and slide it down into position. (Dusting the leg lightly with talcum powder may help prevent the skin from being irritated.) Fasten the fasteners from top to bottom, then check to be sure that none is tighter or looser than the others. Boots must be snug and securely fastened, but not tight enough to interfere with circulation or normal movement. You should be able to slip a finger between the boot and the leg.

Check the tightness of the boots after the horse has been moving for 5 minutes or so. If his legs were a little bit filled or stocked up, they may go down with exercise, which loosens the fastenings.

Boots fastened with single Velcro closures, or those used for galloping and jumping, should be reinforced with strips of tape applied in a spiral. In wet conditions, use plastic tape, not masking tape.

CARE OF BOOTS

Boots must be kept clean and supple. A stiff, dirty boot can irritate the skin or rub a sore on the horse's leg. Proper care will also preserve the boots and prevent them from deteriorating.

Types of protective boots.

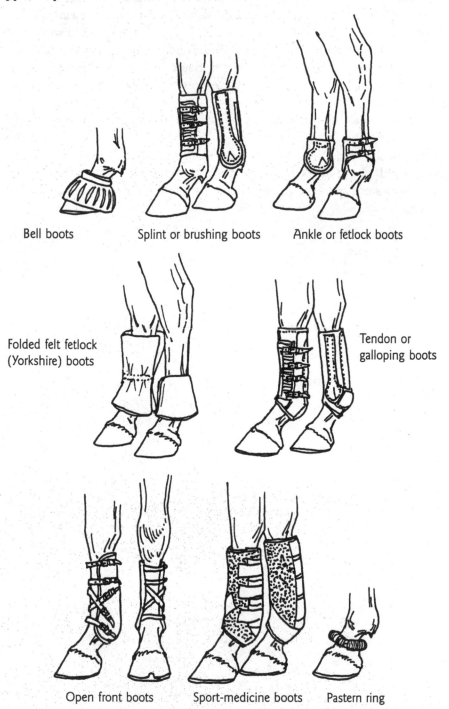

Bell boots   Splint or brushing boots   Ankle or fetlock boots

Folded felt fetlock (Yorkshire) boots   Tendon or galloping boots

Open front boots   Sport-medicine boots   Pastern ring

Boots should be cleaned immediately after use. Wet mud should be rinsed off; dried mud may be removed by brushing. Leather parts should be cleaned with a minimum of water, oiled or conditioned if necessary, then soaped well. Fully waterproof boots may be hosed off or rinsed clean in a bucket of water, but those with leather parts should not be immersed. Some fabric and synthetic boots are machine washable. Fasten the Velcro closures before washing, so they do not pick up dirt and lint.

Boot fastenings are important, as a boot that comes loose during work may trip the horse and cause a fall. Velcro closures should be cleaned periodically with a pin or a large needle, as they lose their ability to grip when they become clogged with dirt or lint. Check the stitching and condition of straps, buckles, and other fastenings frequently, and have them replaced if they become worn or weakened.

Printed in the USA
CPSIA information can be obtained
at www.ICGtesting.com
JSHW012017140824
68134JS00025B/2466

9 780876 056387